STRANGE TALES ABOUT ANIMALS

Weird Wacky and Totally True

by Carole Gerber

illustrated by
Rose Ann Tisserand & Greg Huculak

To Jessica

Published by Willowisp Press, Inc.
10100 SBF Drive, Pinellas Park, Florida 34666

Copyright © 1992 Willowisp Press, Inc.

All rights reserved. No portion of this book may be reproduced, stored in a retrieval system, or transmitted, in any form or by any means, electronic, mechanical, photocopying, recording or otherwise without prior written permission from the publisher.

Printed in the United States of America

2 4 6 8 10 9 7 5 3 1

ISBN 0-87406-632-8

Contents

Practically Perfect...4

And the Answer Is 7

Trick for Treat!...10

Worth Every Penny 14

Now That's Talent!..18

Get In the Swim 22

Best Friends...26

The Star Treatment 30

Practically Perfect

P.C. Reece is practically perfect. He likes to snuggle up and eat popcorn while he watches TV. He's friendly and neat. Does he sound like someone you'd like to know?

P.C.'s only fault is that he eats too much.

Mrs. Reece helps him watch his weight. She feeds P.C. lots of fruits and vegetables. He likes applesauce, broccoli, and bananas. Another favorite food is cottage cheese.

Do you like to be hugged? So does P.C.! But he squeals and runs away if someone tries to pick him up.

Luckily, not many people try because P.C.—short for Pork Chop—weighs 50 pounds. He's a Vietnamese potbellied pig who lives, eats, and watches TV in Columbus, Ohio.

Weird Bit:

Vietnamese potbellied pigs are becoming popular pets. Like cats, they can even be trained to use litter boxes.

Weird Yuk:

Q: What kind of stories do pigs tell?
A: Pig tales!

And the Answer Is...

Hans seemed to be a math genius. He lived in Berlin, Germany, and few people there could stump him on arithmetic questions. Hans became famous!

One day a scientist named Oskar came to test Hans. Right away, Oskar noticed something important. Hans always gave the right answer when the person asking the question knew it, too. But if the questioner didn't know the correct answer, Hans also missed it. What was going on here?

Oskar watched Hans closely. He figured out that Hans got his answers by "reading" people's minds.

That's pretty amazing because Hans was a horse! He tapped out his answers with his hoof!

Weird Bit:

Hans lived nearly 100 years ago. He didn't really read people's minds. He watched their faces and bodies. When he tapped to the right answer, they began to smile. They also leaned toward Hans. Sometimes they sighed with relief. The people didn't know they were giving away the answers. But Hans did. He was one smart horse!

Weird Yuk:

Q: If you find a horseshoe, what does it mean?

A: A poor horse somewhere is going barefoot.

Trick for Treat!

Paul was a tricky youngster who grew up in the country. There were no stores in his neighborhood, and getting food wasn't easy.

One day he saw a grown-up named Mellie digging in the ground. Paul knew tasty things grew there. He also knew he wasn't strong enough to get them himself, and he didn't think Mellie would share.

Suddenly, Paul had an idea.

Paul cried out for his mother. She came running! She thought Mellie had hurt Paul, and she wanted to punish her.

Paul's trick worked. While his mother was chasing Mellie, he ate the plant root Mellie had dropped. Then he calmly wiped his paws.

Paul wasn't very nice. But no one would ever call him a silly baboon!

Weird Bit:

The scientists who watched Paul in Africa say his trickery is common among wild animals. They say animals are smarter than we think—especially when it comes to survival.

Weird Yuk:

Q: If six baboons at a time were chasing you, what time would it be?

A: Six after one.

Worth Every Penny

Polly Cromer had a pain in her stomach. Even though she didn't complain, George Cromer took her to see Dr. Eric Heitman. Dr. Heitman said Polly's pain came from stones that had formed in her kidneys.

Most of the time, doctors cut open the patient's stomach to remove kidney stones.

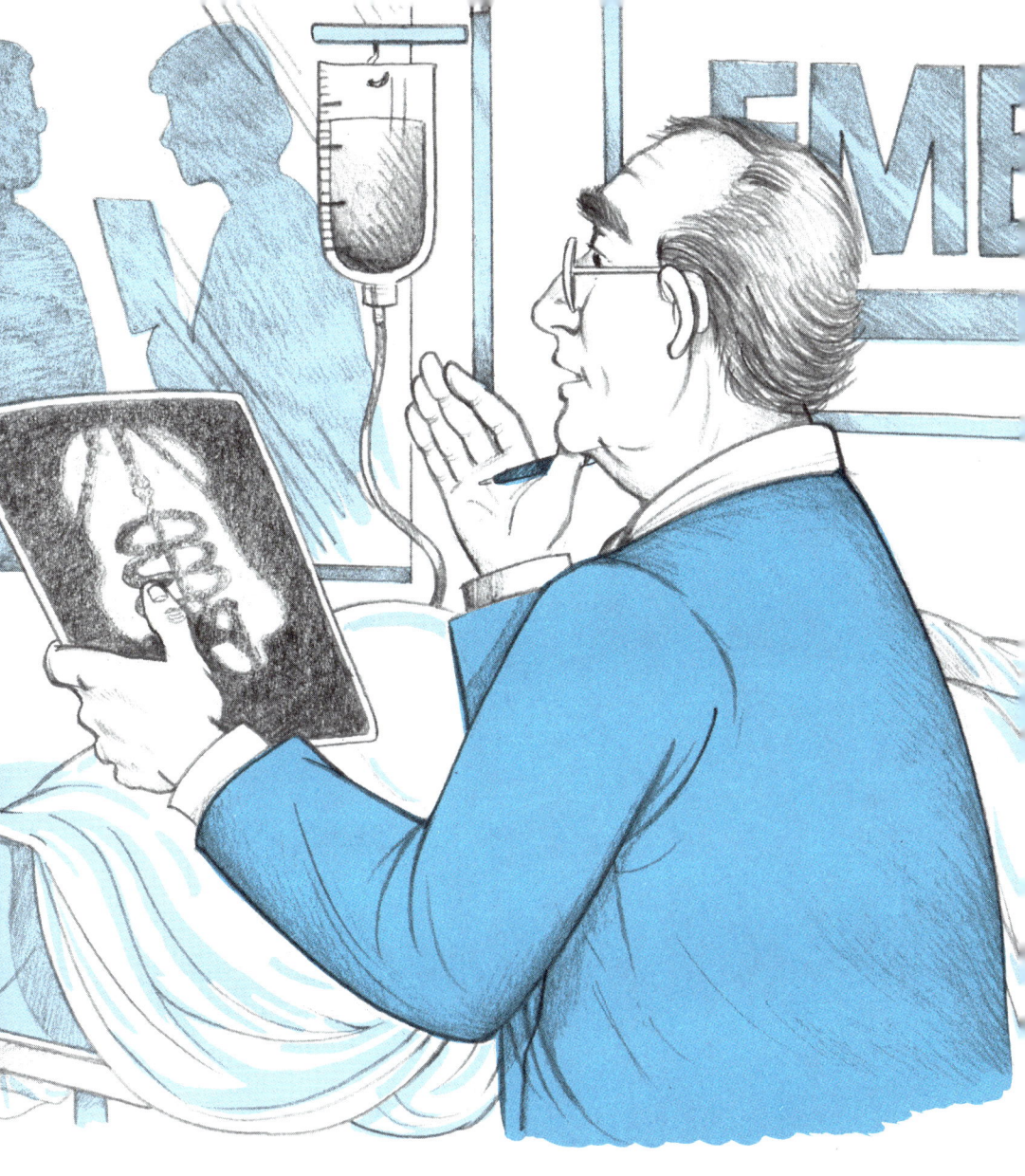

But Dr. Heitman said Polly wasn't strong enough for that. He said Polly should have her stones crushed with a new kind of machine. The machine uses sound waves, which don't hurt.

There was still a big problem left. Using the machine was very expensive.

Luckily, another doctor, Henry Wise, said he would use his machine to crush Polly's stones—for free!

Why? Because Dr. Wise loved dogs and Polly was a beautiful English bulldog. She became the first dog ever to use the special machine, which cost more than a million dollars. Polly must have been worth every penny!

Weird Bit:

Kidney stones are rare in animals. That's why veterinarians like Dr. Heitman don't own the costly machines. Polly's kidney stones were crushed at the Ohio Kidney Stone Center in 1988.

Weird Yuk:

Q: Which pet is always underfoot?
A: The carpet!

Now That's Talent!

Siri was not much to look at. But her fans didn't know that. All they ever saw were her drawings. No one knew exactly what they were. But everyone agreed they were great!

"The lines are so graceful!" said one artist. "They are beautiful," remarked another. An art teacher said Siri's drawings showed she had a gentle nature. A famous artist named Willem de Kooning thought Siri's work had style. Everyone wanted to meet the talented new artist.

Would you like having famous people swoon over your drawings? Most young artists would be thrilled. But not Siri!

She knew her work was solid. It had to be. Siri weighed 8,000 pounds, about average for Asian elephants.

Weird Bit:

Siri was her own art teacher. But she couldn't have developed her talent without some help. Siri lived at the Burnet Park Zoo in Syracuse, New York. In 1980, her keeper saw her draw on the ground with a stick. He gave her pencils, brushes, paints, and paper. Siri created more than 200 pictures!

Weird Yuk:

Q: Where do elephants store their art supplies?

A: In their trunks!

Get In the Swim

Luther is an independent fellow. It's been years since his mother, Lily, told this Florida teen what to do.

Luther enjoys his freedom. Every winter, he takes off alone for Blue Spring State Park near Orange City, Florida. The area is beautiful! He spends most of his time there

with Merlin and Nick. It seems strange, but these guys don't camp out. And no one has ever seen them hike. Instead, they spend all their time at the park's beach.

There, Luther and his friends frolic in the warm water. They show off like crazy— without bathing suits! Is this why so many people take pictures of them?

Nope. It's because Luther and his friends—like all manatees—are so doggone cute!

Weird Bit:

Manatees are gentle, air-breathing mammals that live in the water. They grow to about 10 feet long and can weigh as much as a large horse. Each manatee eats about 100 pounds of water plants daily. Manatees are endangered animals. About 1,200 of them are left. Like Luther, many make their homes in the protected waters of Blue Spring State Park. Scientists there gave them names so they could track their movements.

Weird Yuk:

Q: Why did the manatee sit on a pumpkin?
A: He wanted to play squash.

Best Friends

When Donald Kellogg was a baby, he had a best friend named Gua. Donald and Gua played peek-a-boo indoors. Later, they

played tag outside Donald's home in Orange Park, Florida. Sometimes they pulled each other in a red wagon. They spent almost all their time together.

Donald's father was a scientist. One day he tested Donald and Gua to see what each could do. Gua could run faster than Donald. She could build block towers, too.

But Mrs. Kellogg grew worried about Donald. He spoke only three words. Instead of talking like a normal toddler, Donald grunted. Gua understood him—but no one else did.

Mr. Kellogg returned Gua to the place that had been her home in the beginning—a research center where scientists studied animals. Donald missed his playmate. But he stopped grunting like a chimpanzee. With Gua gone, Donald began talking like a normal child.

Weird Bit:

Gua never learned to talk like people do, but she did figure out ways to get her point across. When she wanted a drink, she stuck out her lips. When she wanted something else, she pulled on a person's hand and grunted.

Weird Yuk:

Q: What do chimpanzees have that no other animal has?

A: Baby chimpanzees!

The Star Treatment

Have you ever wondered what it's like to be a TV star? You can be sure it's exciting! One famous TV star we know flies only first class. The flight attendants pay lots of

attention to him. On breakfast flights, they serve his favorite food—glazed donuts. This TV star is handsome and polite, but kind of weird. No matter how warm it gets on the plane, he won't take off his coat.

Another strange thing: This star never talks to anyone. But the flight attendants don't mind.

Meeting Lassie is too exciting for words. Woof!

Weird Bit:

Since 1954 when the TV series began, six different male dogs have played the role of Lassie—even though Lassie was always portrayed as a female dog!

Weird Yuk:

Q: Why does Lassie wag his tail?
A: Because no one will do it for him.